MEMOIR AS CONVERSATION

Poems by Mark Fleckenstein

For information contact:
Unsolicited Press
Portland, Oregon
www.unsolicitedpress.com
orders@unsolicitedpress.com
619-354-8005

Cover Design: Kathryn Miller
Editor: S.R Stewart

ISBN: 978-1-947021-86-0

MEMOIR AS CONVERSATION

Poems by Mark Fleckenstein

A LOST DIAGRAM OF MARRIAGE

Hands fainting, knees crushed, a French kiss
pummeling the heart. Days go on

like flat tires, smelling of unwashed dries.
A duel of sighs, expectorated breaths, the telephone

just not ringing. The leftovers I sawed off from last night:
night birds, unruly cars, the sound of voices

like foreign intrigue, hand in suspicious hand,
we remain. The bark of unwanted money, a rumor about

children, four square and solemn. Mad
about the boy, mad about the girl, simply

mad together about each other, just a reunion away.

DOING THE SAME THING TWICE

A one-armed conversation. This is the blind side,
absolutely honest and one time before,

erased. Ghosts, with impeccable vocal cords,
so long ago gone, the very light

on their shadow, a pure invention, still can't sing.
Another chance? Your choice: well done

or misbegotten? Somewhere, someone takes the 5th.

HOURGLASS-MEMORY

The once-perfect and perfumed man's image
etched against a mirror,

but not as dead as he should be. The others?
The misremembered, the lonely unto death,

the abandoned, the invisibly hurt, all harshly
eliminated. Memory like an hourglass,

a long, slow accumulation, grain by grain.

MEMOIR AS CONVERSATION

Lucid, lurid dreams, all shiny, and just shy of rage,
tactically misremembered. A piece of moon

lay on the earth. Thinking how long, how hard,
ill-timed, cracked along a fault. Light, a dim

companion. As if what we know might save us.

PHOTOGRAPHIC NEGATIVE

Longing is a kind of hopscotch. Numbered, orderly,
finite, unquestioning. But not the heart:

disheveled, abstracted, necessarily ragged, prone
to miscounting misremembering.

Anatomically closer to the soul, a complicated
warrior, and all for that one, unmerciful

thought, a year in dog bites, nipping at the heels.

WHEN NO DOESN'T REALLY MEAN ANYTHING

After beating your head against the wall
well beyond what's reasonable,

what do you take me for? An alternate model, down
to the cheap make-up, unintentionally

blackened eyes and very dead white rose? If it's
games you like, the board and other

pieces are missing. And you are looking at me
without my head, trapped, rapid fire, in

several unspeakable languages played by ear. If you
ever find what you're looking for, send

me a postcard, an invitation. We'll make it a party.

THINKING OF WHAT'S MISSING

12 years carrying the same bag of eggs (not
in Roman numerals), Playing the changes,

one-off then out, trying to ingest the sun a
few rays and clouds at a time. What

do you know? Replacing your heart for one
with a hole in it, and several stories

meant to cover it, this is how it goes. Invisible,
lighter, improbable, a shadow's memory.

From here take the next open door, anywhere.

PLAYING FOR CHANGE

Changes are miracles. No matter what size
and religion make them into. Star

gnawed, dusty, omnivorous like time or light
flailing around the room, a warming absence.

A room, almost able to sustain light, and whatever
else moves, sloth-slow, silent. Broken, sevened.

Never more than 5 words between it and creation.
A hard sell even for God,

who plays dice, just to annoy Einstein.

TAKING BACK THE NIGHT

Thinking of you, years worn badly. A broken
window here, an improperly hung door,

soiled carpet. Not the same nighttime
"shoot-em up" play as before, but

not all the shots are yours. It's not about
fending off but fixing the frame.

Can several years, decades after passing,
still take a mulligan? I've got you

covered. I'm ready or not.
Come fuck me. Like, again.

The nights have grown shabby, smiling
like only you might,

like a sow eating her young.

A MISTAKE IN LOGIC

Seduced by reason, the third thought
of every word. Learned responses

like forced music, stylish (breathe in, breath out),
bigger and bigger, gin-softened

like mother's milk. and the video that goes
with it. But what for baby? Surprises.

But for now, empty bags, a live animal or two,
a smile from outside. The wind's stuck

on a nail like photographed silence, not trying
to escape or catch up. A short-handed

paradise that no one can actually ignore. A deck
of cards won't make it any better.

Sometimes, someone's hell is diabolically
just like yours, but with more candles,

and music you hate. Anywhere you go,
is the same as where you left,

reasonably or not. The stars never quite really lie.

ADULTS ARE NOT ALWAYS RIGHT, JUST NEVER WRONG

An obsession like a 12-year old, willful, meandering,
hormonal, and like fish, three days

later, staring to smell. An abscess of wisdom teeth,
inaccurately named, necessary to remove.

If you walk the other way, downwind, collar turned
skyward, who'll notice? A concept like freedom,

what do you mean and there you go.

DESPAIR DOESN'T NECESSARILY MEAN SAD

Weepingly in the dark, the telephone not
needing to be answered, the front

door and all windows, safe and unlocked.
At least, a cup's worth of coffee

cooling on the carpet, creamed and sugared
to taste. If the night were to embrace

you, shave away your tears, argue with why
sadness is usually called dark,

no empathy, mistakes despair for reason, bodily
thoughts and memories, imponderable

and trying so hard to make understanding.

THE MAGIC OF CHILDHOOD AND ITS OTHER

The same childhood twice, missing numbers 1 and 2,
the same sledgehammer, empty box imagination,

learning to smoke, innocence of two minds, one
disappeared, forgotten and immolated.

Then again, the one price tag free, no evil. Embraced
always, a soft, protected landing always,

nothing broken, no bones, nothing stolen, no bedtime
games meaning naked, gone awry,

not away. Winter all over the room, escaping its
overcoat, resting on the bed. Two stories, mismatched.

Never accept, or believe only
deny, the bad news.

A wronged mirrors' retelling, remaking something true.

DREAM-MEMORY – (One More Descriptive History of Memory)

From the ash of his last cigarette, a glass and perfumed world,
5, 12, 47 years later, and still

not as dead as he should be. The others? The misremembered,
the lonely unto death, the abandoned,

the invisibly hurt, all harshly eliminated. Memory like an
hourglass, a long and slow accumulation,

grain by grain, almost always wrong and, also painfully true.

WHAT 11:11 REALLY MEANS

He is, in a way, happy: not mesmerized by the ordinary
relived celebration, the --hit or miss tone singing --

softly growing lights, a room missing sleep.
No cars drip passed.

Nothing a knife or God could correct.

A LESSON IN DARKNESS

What one hand doesn't forget, the other doesn't either.
Rules don't work in bedtime games

or chance. Two handed gently pillow reinforced
silence. Thought meaning flesh, refreshed

knowing of what darkness means, led by the hand.

A SIN EATER'S BLESSING

A three-day absence of crows, birth
from a tipped womb forecast my inheritance.

Clothes dirt bloodied, red dirt caked on my lips.
Rawed by longing, an embracable flaw.

Skin against the wind, while death argues
immortality through rotted teeth,

its slit-voice, almost audible. A ticklish situation.
And so you, two cards shy of any blessing.

Encumbered light cast about, believed redemptive,
and easy on the eyes. The house

pouring a candle where it thinks God must sleep.

WE'RE ALL IN OUR PLACES, WITH SMILES ON OUR FACES

Television faces recite color-bright stories of awe
and awful. Almost audible

trauma witnesses become, animated cardboard
stand-ins, hand-fed with the right words.

Knowing how to get there (left from right, a compass's
magnetic points: North, East, South, West)

helps, but only to one train wreck at a time.

DELIVERY BY DAY'S END

Light oaring through a still-born room, completely white
and nearly as quieted. Warm from absence,

conversational jet trails linger.
Just a day, nothing spectacular,

fainting from desire or first aid instructions.
Simple, simply packaged,

non-descript, something every household needs.

ONE BEFORE BED, ONE IN THE MORNING

Pill begot pill, begot pill, begot pill, begot pill,
until the medicine cabinet looked

like a maternity ward, but less noisy, less nosy.
Another mathematical romance of I's, 2's,

many. Resistant to prying, lascivious eyes,
conversational wrong turns

as if there's a miracle nearby.

SOMETIMES THINGS DON'T LOOK LIKE WHAT THEY ARE

Chance lightning, a form of love, usually mistaken for
a host of intimate diseases, and not

as believable as ball-lightning. A hot and icy self-consuming
leftover blue light. Lasts a day, sometimes

a week, but not exactly. It's better to hide,
keeping expectations low,

close to the ground like already cut grass.

ON NOT PRAYING

What happened was.
Was as is is, was, will and will

not. Right, wrong, color voided, all
in agreement like cut flowers

arranged for Mother's and Father's Day.

AN EVERYDAY CONUNDRUM

The first crow in a field,
a pearl of the dark, claims it.

Then night, morning and other weather.
The crow remains like a philosopher's first question.

When it leaves, the air fills in mostly.

CHANCE MEETING

Ironic as a circle.
Ending and beginning the same blink.

Always two halves of the same
compliment, conflict.

Not an exaggeration of feeling,
a bird mistaking a window for air,

or of fact, lightning in the next room,
but the other one.

The soul and its magnifying glass.

IF WALLS COULD SEE, WHAT WOULD IT BE

Punch-drunk voices, too tired for language,
burrow through the room next door.

Like what a nail, if able to speak, might complain
about. Being struck, stuck. The argument

after. Limited to a single ongoing dream.
That day and night could be twins.

Wishing, not an anticipation, just a bent, slivered wish.

TRYING TO GET IT RIGHT

Rise Up. There are more stories, buried water, rock-
salt and entangled ears.

Rise up. Beyond snow, dimpled light, waiting
for something uncertain, a delivery.

Some years are like that. Waiting, cured of light. Most are.

About the Author

Mark Fleckenstein was born in Chicago, and grew up in Ohio, Michigan, Connecticut, North Carolina, and New Hampshire. He graduated from University of North Carolina in Charlotte with a B.A. in English, Vermont College of Fine Arts and received an MFA in Writing. He's became very involved in the poetry community in and around Boston, for over 30 years. He was an assistant editor for *(BLuR)*, *the Boston Literary Review*, founder/coordinator of two bi-weekly poetry reading series in Boston and a workshop leader, He's given poetry readings with famous poets (Charles Simic, Linda Gregg, Mark Doty, Mark Cox and Carl Phillips) and not so famous poets. Six states and dozens of moves later, he settled in Massachusetts. He is also a painter. He has two amazing daughters and a large, eccentric, long-haired black cat named Ariadne.

About the Press

Unsolicited Press was founded in 2012 and is based in Portland, Oregon. Comprised of dedicated volunteers, the press published award-winning authors in all genres.

Learn more at unsolicitedpress.com.